Taiko
MASTER

Rob Waring, *Series Editor*

HEINLE
CENGAGE Learning

Australia • Brazil • Japan • Korea • Mexico • Singapore • Spain • United Kingdom • United States

Words to Know

This story is set in the United States (U.S.). It happens in San Francisco [sæn frənsɪskoʊ], California, near the Pacific Ocean.

 Taiko Drumming. Read the paragraph. Then match each word with the correct definition.

Taiko drumming is an ancient Japanese art, but it is also done in Western countries. 'Taiko' is a Japanese word which means 'drum'. These musical instruments make loud noises when taiko drummers beat them. They use drumsticks to do this. Taiko drumming is difficult and the drummers must practise so they can improve. They practise in a special place called a 'dojo'. If a person works very hard, he or she may become a grand master of taiko.

1. drum _____	**a.** hit again and again
2. beat _____	**b.** a stick for hitting a drum
3. drumstick _____	**c.** someone who performs an art at the highest level
4. practise _____	**d.** a Japanese word for 'practice place'
5. *dojo* _____	**e.** do something again and again to get better at it
6. grand master _____	**f.** a round musical instrument hit with hands or sticks

Taiko Drummers

2

B **In the *Dojo*.** Read the definitions. Complete the paragraph with the correct form of the words.

mind: the part of a person that allows them to think and feel
sensei: Japanese word which means 'teacher'
warrior: fighter
traditional: done for a long time by a particular society or group

Many Japanese arts are practised in a 'dojo'. A *dojo* is a place where people can practise (1)_____ Japanese arts. *Dojos* have a long history. They are the places where many strong Japanese (2)_____ practised and became very good fighters. In a *dojo*, there is always a (3)_____, or teacher, who helps the students improve. The students have to work hard with both their bodies and their (4)_____.

Warriors Fighting in an Ancient Dojo

Two thousand years ago, Japanese warriors used drums to make their **enemies**[1] fear them. In ancient Japan, the drum was very important in everyday life, too. People used to mark village **boundaries**[2] by how far the sounds of drums travelled. People even used to do their daily activities to the beat of drums. However, slowly over the years, the sound of the drums went away – until now.

---

[1]**enemy:** a person or group that wants to hurt another
[2]**boundary:** the point where one thing ends and another begins

Japanese warriors used drums to make their enemies afraid.

Now, far away from Japan, in the United States, a new **audience**[3] is listening to this ancient drum. The art is called 'taiko', and it has come from the villages of Japan to the city of San Francisco.

One drummer explains an important part of taiko is that a group of individual drummers must act as one. "The **essence**[4] of taiko is that it's not just people drumming," she says. "It's the **unity**[5] of drummers amongst themselves."

---

[3]**audience:** people who come together to listen to and watch an event
[4]**essence:** basic meaning
[5]**unity:** coming together; feeling of being one

In San Francisco, the movement of the body has now been added to traditional taiko drumming. It is now an art form that brings together sound, body, and mind. During a performance, the energy of all of these parts goes into the beating of the drums.

Identify the Main Idea

1. What is the main idea of the paragraph?

2. What would be a better heading for this page?
   a. 'Traditional Taiko Drumming'
   b. 'Taiko Combines Sound, Body, and Mind'

Some ancient arts have added body movement to bring together sound, body and mind.

Taiko Grand Master Seiichi Tanaka explains what happens when the drummer and drum unite. According to him, it's almost as if the drum and drummer become one. "Your self and the drum, totally get together. Into the drum, your self," he says as he moves his body forward, "... and [the] drum [comes] to you," he adds as he moves his body back. "Both [are] **mutual**,[7]" he explains.

---

[7]**mutual:** equal or similar

Scan for Information

Scan pages 12-15 to find the information.

1. When did Seiichi Tanaka come to the U.S.?

2. In which two countries did Seiichi Tanaka start taiko drumming?

3. How many groups are there now in the two countries?

In the early 1900s, traditional taiko was very popular in Japanese-American communities. However, by the mid 1900s, many people were losing interest in taiko drumming. Then, in 1968, Seiichi Tanaka arrived and brought new interest and a new style of drumming from Japan. After that, things changed. Tanaka explains: "I was just **fresh off the boat**,"[8] he says, "so [a] whole bunch of 'fresh off the boat' people [got] together and play[ed] drums."

---

[8]**fresh off the boat:** *(slang)* new to a place or experience

Tanaka is also known as 'Tanaka Sensei' to his students in the *dojo*. They know that he is an important man in taiko. They also realise that he is responsible in part for its popularity in North America. "Tanaka Sensei is a real **pioneer**,"[9] says one student. "He's made a **dozen**[10] or so groups in the sixties and seventies, into something like eight hundred groups now spread all over this country and Canada."

[9] **pioneer:** one of the first people to do something
[10] **dozen:** twelve of something

What makes taiko special? According to Tanaka Sensei and other taiko drummers, it's all about the feeling of energy. "All energy from **Mother Nature**[11] [goes] through your body, come[s] to my body – here" Tanaka says, pointing to his arm. He then adds, "[it] go[es] through to the drumstick – BAM!" he says, as he moves his drumstick quickly.

One student explains that taiko drummers sometimes have to play through pain and tiredness while practising or performing. At that point, he says that they can really express their feelings and energy. According to him, "it's almost as if you are standing outside of your body kind of looking in…and you hit this point where you're just completely free."

---

[11] **Mother Nature:** the imaginary mother of all things

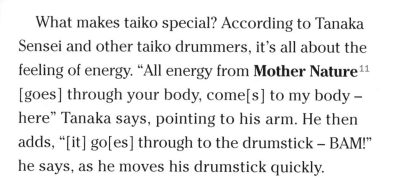

Another drummer also feels that taiko is about giving energy. "The essence of taiko is giving your 110 percent," she says. "You have to always give, because if you don't give, and everyone else is giving, then you're **draining**[12] from them."

Here in San Francisco, taiko came from the old world of Japan and was born again. Grand Master Seiichi Tanaka has given North America the chance to enjoy the energy and excitement of traditional taiko drumming.

---

[12] **drain:** take away; use up

After You Read

1. Japanese warriors used their drums to make their enemies _____.
   A. approach
   B. fight
   C. leave
   D. mark

2. On page 4, the word 'mark' can be replaced by:
   A. touch
   B. want
   C. research
   D. determine

3. On page 7, the drummer believes that an important part of taiko is:
   A. the group experience
   B. the individual drummers
   C. the ancient drums
   D. the audience

4. The new form of taiko is from San Diego.
   A. True
   B. False

5. On page 8, 'it' refers to:
   A. movement
   B. sound
   C. new taiko
   D. tradition

6. Sound, _____, and _____ are brought together in this new form of taiko.
   A. tradition, beating
   B. body, mind
   C. performance, mind
   D. body, energy

7. How do the drummer and drum become one?
   A. The energy of playing brings them together.
   B. The drum touches the drummer.
   C. Seiichi Tanaka unites with the drum.
   D. The movement brings together all drummers.

8. What's the main idea on page 12?
   A. Drumming on boats
   B. Traditional taiko came from the U.S.
   C. Tanaka brought a new drumming style
   D. People aren't interested in Taiko

9. On page 15, 'sixties and seventies' refers to:
   A. the number of drummers
   B. the time between 1960 and 1979
   C. the age of the drummers
   D. the number of drums

10. Tanaka Sensei thinks that Taiko drumming is special because of the:
    A. energy
    B. drumsticks
    C. imaginary drums
    D. Japanese drums

11. Taiko drummers have to play through _____ and _____.
    A. energy, freedom
    B. pain, expression
    C. pain, tiredness
    D. energy, tiredness

12. What is the purpose of this story?
    A. To introduce the grand masters of Japan
    B. To talk to drummers about old and new taiko
    C. To present old and new Japan
    D. To introduce an energetic drumming style

http://www.interesting*scotland.com.uk

Scotland's African Drum Village

Most people think of Scotland as a quiet place with fields and farm animals, but did you know that Scotland has a lot more to offer? In recent years, Dundee, Scotland's fourth-largest city, has become a centre for the arts. Few people think of Scotland as a place to hear African drumming. However, just north of Dundee, there is an African drumming programme that attracts a large audience. People come to this event from all over the world.

African Drum Village is a five-day meeting between drummers and people who enjoy the excitement of drumming. It is the first and only meeting of its kind in Scotland. Some of the best drummers

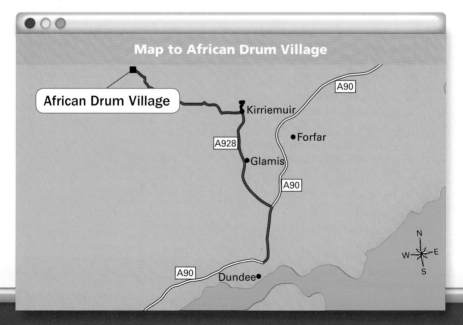

Map to African Drum Village

African Drum Village

Kirriemuir

A90

A928

Forfar

Glamis

A90

A90

Dundee

N
W E
S

in the world attend the programme. There is something for everyone at African Drum Village. As a visitor, you can listen to wonderful performances from grand masters. Beginners can also have drumming lessons with the masters. More experienced drummers can form drumming groups with others. African Drum Village is a spiritual event for many visitors. It is their chance to connect with nature and discover new music. The beauty of Scotland and the skill of the drummers ensure that visitors have a wonderful experience.

This year musician and teacher Famoudou Konaté is the main attraction at African Drum Village. Mr. Konaté is a grand master of drumming in the ancient Malinké Djembe tradition. He was born in 1940 in Guinea in Africa. By the time he was 14 years old, his drumming was already well known throughout Africa. For the last 40 years, Konaté has performed in Europe, the United States, and many other parts of the world. African Drum Village is very pleased to present Mr. Konaté this year.

A Visitor Enjoying African Drum Village

Word Count: 326
Time: _____

Vocabulary List

audience (7)

beat (2, 4, 8)

boundary (4)

dojo (2, 3, 15)

dozen (15)

drain (19)

drum (2, 4, 5, 7, 8, 11, 12, 16, 19)

drumstick (2, 16)

enemy (4)

essence (7, 19)

fresh off the boat (12)

grand master (2, 11, 19)

mind (3, 8, 9)

Mother Nature (16)

mutual (11)

pioneer (15)

practise (2, 3, 16)

sensei (3, 15)

traditional (3, 8, 12)

unity (7)

warrior (3, 4, 5)